Advance Praise for *Heart Dog*!

"*Heart Dog* does an amazing job of capturing and exploring the personal, and often indescribable, feelings of grief and loss that come with the death of a treasured pet. This book is a great resource for anyone currently grieving the loss of their Heart Dog."

— Dr. Stacy D. Meola, veterinarian and board-certified veterinary emergency and critical care specialist (Heart Dog, Casey – December 24, 2009)

"Roxanne Hawn has the rare gift of melding emotion and logic in good writing. She offers the practical advice of dealing with the day-by-day, step-by-step acceptance of the loss of a Heart Dog. Never preachy, never judgmental, this book offers the reader tools and the space to deal with the emptiness of losing a best friend."

— Leland Dirks, author of *Seven Dogs in Heaven*

"A hopeful, encouraging read. *Heart Dog* is like having your best friend put their arm around your shoulder and tell you everything's going to be OK."

— Peggy Frezon, author of *Faithfully Yours* (Heart Dog, Brooks – April 6, 2013)

"Honest, concise, and ultimately hopeful, veteran author and dog-lover Roxanne Hawn has transformed the deep pain of losing her canine soul mate, Lilly, into an empathetic guide that provides wisdom and comfort to any of us who have experienced the loss of a much beloved pet. Balancing her own story with those shared by her readers, Hawn walks the reader through the painful process of loss from the early stages of grief through the memorials that help us heal. So many people struggling with their feelings ask themselves, 'Am I alone in feeling this way?' and 'Will I ever get better?' *Heart Dog* will assure them, with candor and compassion, the answers — in order — are 'No' and 'Yes.'"

– Dr. Jessica Vogelsang, veterinarian and author of *All Dogs Go to Kevin* (Heart Dog, Emmett – July 21, 2009)

"Some dogs come into our lives for a reason. When that reason also brings heartbreak, the road ahead may seem impossible. *Heart Dog* gives you fresh ideas for working through your grief."

– Dr. Rainier Ko, veterinarian and board-certified veterinary neurologist, neurosurgeon, surgeon (Heart Dog, Belle – September 11, 1995)

"When I lost my Heart Dog, luckily I had a few long-distance friends who knew what I was going through, and they were an immense help. If you're experiencing the shock and devastation of losing your canine soul mate, and none of your friends and family seem to understand, Roxanne Hawn's words in *Heart Dog* can be that long-distance friend that you need. Told from the vantage point of her own devastating grief, along with input from a survey of 500 others who've lost their Heart Dogs, the book helps you understand what to expect in the coming days, weeks, months, and more as you slog through your grief and find your new normal. *Heart Dog* would make a great gift, for yourself or a loved one suffering the profound loss of a Heart Dog."

– Jackie Bouchard, USA Today bestselling author of *Rescue Me, Maybe*
(Heart Dog, Abby – January 10, 2012)

"Roxanne's experience mirrored so many of my own emotions I felt after losing my Maltese, Angel, nearly 20 years ago. Having had multiple dogs throughout my life, I really hadn't considered any of them a Heart Dog until remembering my grief over Angel. I wish I had this book then."

– Kerri Fivecoat-Campbell, author of *Living Large in our Little House: Thriving in 480-Square Feet with Six Dogs, a Husband and One Remote* (Heart Dog, Angel – April 28, 1996)

"Roxanne Hawn has written a poignant book that should appeal to anyone who has suffered significant loss in their life, in particular the death of their Heart Dog. Roxanne relates her own experiences with severe grief, and personal struggles, following the death of her Heart Dog, Lilly. She offers the reader numerous valuable insights, along with thoughtful advice for understanding and trying to cope with such a momentous private hurt. As a veterinarian, I highly recommend this book to any member of the veterinary medical health care team, who would like to gain knowledge and understanding regarding the strong feelings and severe stresses, which their clients may undergo, following the loss of a beloved pet, specifically their Heart Dog.

– Dr. Ted Cohn, veterinarian and American Veterinary Medical Association president 2014-15

"You might feel alone in your grieving over your Heart Dog, but you are not. Through the gift of this book, Roxanne Hawn will be by your side every step of the way. She gets it. She has been there, and she will skillfully guide and comfort you through your process. You will realize you belong to a community of people who have had that life-changing experience of living with, loving, and losing a Heart Dog. You will be offered many helpful ideas for how to work with your grief and how to honor your Heart Dog's memory. Most importantly, in Roxanne you will find a friend, a wise and nurturing friend, who knows just how you feel."

– Leslie McDevitt, MLA CDBC CPDT-KA, author of *Control Unleashed* and *Control Unleashed: The Puppy Program*

"When my Luna died after a chronic illness, I was more than devastated. Even though I knew it was inevitable, the loss was overwhelming. I was lost without her. I turned to *Heart Dog: Surviving the Loss of Your Canine Soul Mate*, where I found comfort in learning ways to mitigate the depths of my grief. This insightful book enabled me to grieve in a more healthful way, getting through the mourning roadblocks that so engulfed me. I would recommend it to everyone going through a loss."

– Hilary Lane, dog trainer / owner of Fang Shui Canines (Heart Dog, Luna – February 24, 2015)

"Roxanne Hawn's gentle, supportive, and practical advice is one of the only things getting me through the agonizing recent loss of my own Heart Dog. She has written from the depth of her soul to help others experiencing this terrible grief and her wisdom, coupled with the extensive survey she did of others in this situation, has helped me know I am not alone and that there is a path out of the darkness. I'm reading parts of this deeply insightful book over and over as a lifeline."

– Brette Sember, author / blogger,
BretteSember.com

"I lost my brother and my Heart Dog, Jasmine, a month apart. I confess that the loss of Jasmine struck me harder. I have witnessed the love and bond Roxanne and her Heart Dog, Lilly, shared. I saw their struggles and her pain after Lilly's passing. Roxanne's book offers a beacon of light in the darkness of the terrible grief; a fully loaded first-aid kit for Heart Dog loss survival."

– Jana Rade, blogger / author of *Dawg Business:
It's Your Dog's Health*

Heart Dog
Surviving the Loss of Your Canine Soul Mate

By
Roxanne Hawn

Author of award-winning dog blog
Champion of My Heart

CONTENTS

PREFACE
HOPE FOR THE HEARTBROKEN

I have loved nine dogs in my lifetime. I have grieved seven of them so far. The most recent loss of my Heart Dog in December 2013 is the inspiration for this book. Today and always, I pay homage to Lilly, a Border Collie and the first true canine heroine in my life.

Nothing prepared me for how much worse my grief over losing my Heart Dog would be. Her death feels galaxies more painful than the others did at the time.

The death of any dog is hard. The death of a Heart Dog — a canine soul mate — is much, much worse.

I hope to explain this extreme grief phenomenon and to offer practical ideas for wading through the emotional sludge that comes from losing your Heart Dog.

Yes, I've made some assumptions: Canine soul mates exist. Most people experience a Heart Dog relationship at some point in their lives. The grief when a Heart Dog dies is epic.

If you purchased this book for yourself, I am very sorry for your loss. Even without knowing you or the cause of your dog's passing, I can assure you that you are not alone. Many of us have walked the same road. We've survived the loss. You can too.

If you're giving this book as a gift, I applaud you for recognizing this profound loss in someone else's life. Not everyone gets it, and that lack of empathy compounds the grief people feel. I'm thankful that you understand, and I'm sure the book's recipient will appreciate and remember your kindness.

Inside *Heart Dog: Surviving the Loss of Your Canine Soul Mate,* you'll find real-world strategies from my experiences as well as from 500 others who've faced such grief and took part in an online survey. For some, the loss is recent. For others, it is years in the past.

As the Heart Dog Grief Survey results show, many of us remain standing months and years later, despite the crushing grief.

How recently did you lose your Heart Dog?
- 13% — less than 3 months

- 8% — 3 to 6 months
- 10% — 6 to 12 months
- 20% — 1 to 3 years
- 11% — 3 years
- 38% — more than 3 years

No matter where you are in this process, I send you wishes for peace and comfort.

Quick note: Because my own Heart Dog was female, I use the pronoun *her* throughout the book. It isn't meant to ignore male Heart Dogs. It just seems less contrived to pick a pronoun and stick with it.

Here is an overview of the chapters ahead:

Chapter 1: What Is a Heart Dog?
Defines and discusses the unique bond between people and canine soul mates, including answering the most common questions, including why and how such bonds form.

Chapter 2: Grief Basics and Grief Amplified
Argues for updates to the traditional stages of grief and provides examples of how they might look and feel after the loss of your Heart Dog.

Chapter 3: The Early Days of Grief
Provides coping strategies for getting through the first days, weeks, and months of your loss.

Chapter 4: Small Steps Forward

Outlines ways to balance archiving your Heart Dog's life with other memorial activities.

Chapter 5: Mourning and Memorializing Your Heart Dog

Gives suggestions and directions for creative ways to mourn and memorialize your Heart Dog.

Chapter 6: Comforting Thoughts

Offers comforting practices and parables from a variety of traditions.

Chapter 7: When Grief Gets Worse, Not Better

Addresses the possibility of depression and despair taking root and how to move toward healing.

Chapter 8: Your Next Dog

Discusses the pressures you'll face and things to consider before bringing another dog home.

Chapter 9: Forever Changed

Concludes with a gratitude exercise that honors the magnitude of your loss and the wisdom gained from the experience.

1
WHAT IS A HEART DOG?

When it comes to love,
you either know or you don't.

The term "Heart Dog" means a dog who is your canine soul mate. The phrase serves as shorthand in certain circles of dog lovers to describe the canine love of your life. You just sort of know that your connection to this dog grew into something more than you've felt in the past.

In some cases, no trigger marks a particular dog as your Heart Dog. Sometimes, it's magic, fate, kismet, or dumb luck. Since her death, I've come to think of my Heart Dog, Lilly, as a singularity.

Often, however, this especially strong bond between a dog and a person flourishes in situations that crop up during your time together, such as:

- Canine illness
- Illness(es) in yourself or your family
- Life-changing losses in your family (spouses, parents, children, siblings, friends)
- Children growing up and moving away
- Real-life traumas such as being in a bad car accident together, becoming victims of a crime, or your house burning down
- Major life transitions such as graduations, cross-country moves, marriages, big job changes, or divorces
- Tremendous adventures such as once-in-a-lifetime vacations together, daily traditions, or your dog being in your wedding party

For many years, I wrote about relationships and marriage. That work — including attending more than 24 strangers' weddings a year for six straight years — along with my own life experiences made me believe the following about people and dogs: When it comes to love, you either know or you don't.

Life and Love

Much like I knew my husband was The One when friends and family arranged an unexpected date, I just knew I had an unusual connection with my Heart Dog. Over our nine years together, Lilly and I forged a tremendous partnership across many shared experiences — beginning with the realization of how truly, clinically fearful Lilly was, after what we can only assume was a rough, poorly socialized puppyhood.

Helping Lilly build her confidence began with the usual dog training, where she earned an early first-place obedience trophy by greatly outscoring all the other dogs and puppies on the final exam. We graduated to agility, which Lilly loved as long as there were no other dogs around. That's the main reason we took private lessons, played on our at-home agility course, and never competed in the sport. We also tried rally obedience classes, which are much more relaxed than other kinds of competitive obedience events, but Lilly worried about the other dogs there too. Ultimately, we found a different kind of dog-skills class — held outdoors at a variety of locations. Lilly did better at these outdoor classes. If she needed more space from the other dogs, we could move away or behind a tree. Later on, Lilly and I also played a little at private herding lessons — which Lilly loved. However, not long after we started learning to herd goats, Lilly became sick.

The truth is that a lot of people told me to give up on Lilly and just keep her at home, where she wouldn't be as scared. Lilly absolutely enjoyed a great life at home, but I believed she deserved more.

I treasured and now greatly miss our adventures. Together, Lilly and I took many walks and hikes on countless trails. We rode around town in the car, me singing with the sunroof open. We played fetch so much that I injured my shoulder. I taught Lilly oodles of tricks, most of which she picked up unimaginably fast. We howled together. We sat outside in the summer and snuggled inside in the winter. She kept me company when I worked in the garden. I read or knitted by Lilly's side as she hollowed out bones and food-stuffed toys.

It would be easy to attribute our deep connection to the fact that I work from home, meaning Lilly and I were together nearly 24/7 for nine years, but it's more than that.

At times, it felt like we truly were one.

Perhaps the best example of the extreme value that my Heart Dog added to my life comes from December 30, 2009, about two years before Lilly became sick. Both my mother and her husband were hospitalized. My sister had just come through yet another chemo treatment. On that snowy night, with temps in the low 20s, we could not reach my mother-in-law by phone. We called over and over again. No answer. Because my brother-in-law lived closer — 10 minutes away versus more than 30 for us on bad roads — we called and asked him to check on her. He found her outside, crumpled on the frigid concrete patio, unresponsive.

My husband raced to the emergency room and met the ambulance. His mother's core body temperature was in the 80s, which is dangerously low, life-threatening hypothermia. As the night wore on, and the critical care doctors warmed her body, she awoke and seemed like herself. Oh, there were many surgeries ahead to repair bones shattered from her fall, and we didn't know how much damage the freezing temperatures had done, but she was alive.

Those many hours between finding my mother-in-law in the cold and her surviving that first critical night are a testament to Lilly repaying all the time and energy and care I'd poured into her life over many years. That night, when all my go-to people were unavailable to me — my mom, my sister, my husband — Lilly stayed by my side as I cried, waiting desperately by the phone.

Common Questions About Heart Dogs

On my *Champion of My Heart* dog blog, I posted an online poll in spring 2014, asking people about their Heart Dog experiences. I'll be sharing some insights from that survey throughout the book, but one blog comment stood out.

Someone asked, "Aren't all dogs Heart Dogs?" In a word, no.

Like me, I'm sure you understand the intent of the question. All dogs deserve love. Everyone loves their dogs, all of them, not just one. That's absolutely true. I've loved all the dogs in my life with "my whole heart," as we're fond of saying at my house. Certainly, you have too.

As painful as it can be, I was raised to go "all in" with love — to borrow a poker term. I fall hard. I fall fast, and my loyalty and love are resolute. And, yet, my love for my own Heart Dog eclipses the abiding love I've felt for other dogs.

One of our veterinarians, who lost her own Heart Dog not that long ago and who completely "got me" and where I was in my relationship with Lilly, describes the connection with a Heart Dog as being "pathologically attached."

I love that phrase because there is something right on the cusp of unhealthy about loving a dog so very much.

In response to the survey, someone else asked if the person + Heart Dog relationship must be reciprocal. In other words, is the dog incredibly attached to you as well? It's an interesting question because many people — especially those working in animal rescue — find themselves hopelessly attached to dogs with serious behavior issues that prevent the dogs from returning love in the way a person might hope.

I heard from someone who met her Heart Dog in a veterinary hospital where she worked. Never technically "hers," the woman felt nonetheless that this dog was her Heart Dog, and she grieved accordingly when he died.

Toward the end of my Heart Dog's illness, we joked that her miraculous survival for so long, against so many odds, meant that she clearly was Border Collie + unicorn. The idea stemmed from a tumor that sprouted from her forehead like a unicorn's horn.

I told one of Lilly's veterinary technicians about our Unicorn Dog joke, and she immediately adopted it to mean patients she or others on the veterinary team will always remember.

We hosted a crowdfunding campaign in Lilly's memory after her death. We used the money raised to pay for other dogs' veterinary care. I set no criteria for Lilly's Fund grants, except I really wanted to help other Unicorn Dogs.

The Heart Dog discussion on *Champion of My Heart* also veered into the idea of whether or not a Heart Dog + person relationship was a naturally occurring phenomenon or if it was possible to nurture this kind of super-bond with a dog. My gut tells me that it's a little of both, with maybe a bit more weight on the nature rather than the nurture side.

However, I would never discourage you from spending more time with your dog(s) or from doing many fun or challenging things together to make the bond you already have even stronger. Hike or run together. Swim together. Travel together. Take part in advanced dog training — scent work, dock diving, freestyle (dancing), or whatever makes you both happy. Really, I invite you to participate in activities that forge a stronger partnership and more collaboration with the dogs in your life. Capable of doing and feeling so much more than many people give them credit for, dogs make great friends, teachers, and soul mates.

My point? Heart Dogs do exist. They are special. And, when they die, the grief exceeds expectations.

2
GRIEF BASICS AND GRIEF AMPLIFIED

Canine soul mates exist. The grief over their loss is galaxies beyond what you'd expect.

Plenty of other books and resources explain the five stages of grief, so rather than rehash that information, here is the traditional list of stages that didn't describe my experience at all: denial, anger, bargaining, depression, and acceptance.

Heart Dog grief is worse — epic, in fact. That's one of the assumptions of this book. And it's confirmed by grief survey respondents.

How would you describe your grief over losing your Heart Dog compared to other dogs you've lost?

- 2 times more grief — 14%

- 10 times more grief — 37%
- 100 times more grief — 36%

For 13% of respondents, their Heart Dog marked their first-ever dog loss, so they had nothing with which to compare.

Not Denial, Try Shock

The early days after the loss of a Heart Dog drag, as the pain of grief somehow warps your sense of time and of everything. At my house, life looked and felt blurry. It seemed either too quiet or so loud that I wanted to throw a tantrum, telling everyone to shut up. The seemingly inane nature of normal daily life — especially as revealed on social media — made me want to bash my head on the desk.

Each person's body copes with the flood of grief in different ways. Having eventually lost my mother-in-law in May 2012 and my own mom in June 2013, I was prepared for extreme body chills. What others call denial, I experience as shock. True, honest-to-goodness bodily shock — with all my blood rushing to my core, leaving me shivering and somewhat unable to move. Grief also makes me feel barfy. Even brushing my teeth often brought me to the brink of vomiting.

Your body may react otherwise. Maybe you feel feverish instead of cold. Maybe you wolf down food no problem, but itch all the time. Maybe your heart races. Maybe you get headaches. Maybe your whole body hurts, if for no other reason than full-blown sobbing is hard on muscles and joints.

In my world, grief begins as a profound shock of having a Heart Dog here one minute and gone — gone forever — the next. For me, there was no denial in the early days. Those feelings like "I can't believe she is gone" didn't come until much later.

For me, those first days felt hyper-real. It was all I could do to remain upright amid the black-hole desperation of both heart and soul. I know other people like to keep busy at such a time, and I've done a bit of that too. I tend to clean house or cook when I'm upset. Mostly, however, it took every ounce of strength I had to function somewhat normally. For me, this first crushing time of grief usually lasts four to six weeks before I come out of a deep, dark funk.

Shock probably hits harder if your Heart Dog dies suddenly, as was the case for 52% of our Heart Dog Grief Survey respondents. The other 48% shepherded their Heart Dogs through a longer illness, which brings a whole host of changes and potentially painful memories.

Yes, Anger

On this one, I agree with calling the stage anger. Quite pronounced on arrival, anger raced ahead like a freight train, pulling my heavy load of grief up great hills. Maybe your anger feels more focused, but mine struck out in all directions. I found myself cranky with the world at large. I hated everyone and everything. Not all the time, but my anger surfaced in spurts of extreme frustration and annoyance.

When the anger hits, I recommend avoiding social media for a while. The happy, happy people and the worst-day-ever types will make you boil. Rather than risk ruining friendships by lashing out, better to avoid the venue altogether.

Not Bargaining, Just Regret

What others call bargaining arrived in my grief-stricken life as regret. Three days before Lilly's death, I postponed her euthanasia in consultation with our large team of veterinarians. I believe that was the right decision. Lilly rallied — as she had so many times before — and enjoyed two remarkably good days. Then, on the third day, we found ourselves in an emergency situation that I'd wanted to avoid. There were no last-ditch fixes for the cascade of things going wrong.

I do not regret having Lilly euthanized on Tuesday, December 17, 2013. Instead, I regret that her final day ended up being more desperate than I'd hoped. I didn't want Lilly to be in pain or in fear. It makes me sick to think that she likely experienced both. I had plans for her final moments

— plans forgotten in the urgency of the situation.

The final stage of Lilly's illness came quickly and decisively — leaving us no doubt it was time to let her go. In those early days, I found that swift conclusion both haunting and a blessing. Even now, only the haunted feeling remains. I fear it's a life-long affliction that cannot be fixed, shared, or discussed with anyone — only tolerated.

Keep that in mind when people ask questions you can't or won't answer. Call it discretion or privacy, but no one else is entitled to know the painful details. You owe no one any information about your Heart Dog's death. Talk about it if you want to, but if you don't, know that I support you. There are details I do not talk about with anyone.

You may not feel the kind of hurts-in-your-tummy regret I've experienced. I sincerely hope you don't. For you, the regret may feel more like a doubt or a worry that you made certain decisions too soon or too late. Maybe you question what else you could have done or tried. For some, the regret comes from simply not having local access to a treatment option that may have helped.

I'm not sure if there is a solution to regret, other than believing that you did the best that you could for as long as you could. In the early months, I found this Helen Keller quote of some comfort: "No effort that we make to attain something beautiful is ever lost."

Depression Feels Closer to Desperation

The traditional list of grief stages calls this part of the process depression, and I suppose that works. For me, it felt more like a lingering desperation, with a strong undertow of fear that I might never recover, might never feel better — might actually drop dead of grief. Truly, sometimes the pain is still so great that I fear my heart may simply stop.

From the beginning of grief through this later stage, you may have trouble eating or sleeping. You may feel the urge to exercise all the time or never. At least once, you may worry that you're somehow abnormal because you haven't yet bounced back. In fact, after those early months, the grief only got worse, not better, for me.

Acceptance? Really More Like Soldiering On

The usual list of grief stages ends with acceptance. That word doesn't work for me at all. I accepted my Heart Dog's death from the get-go. Finding a way to go on without her? That's something else entirely.

The truth is that we're never going to be the same after such a profound loss. So, if there is anything to accept, it's understanding that losing your Heart Dog changes you forever. Period.

And that's OK. In fact, sometimes when people ask how I am, I answer simply: "I'm forever changed by the loss." It's accurate. It's true to my experience and honors the tremendous loss, without shortchanging Lilly's memory or, I hope, without making others feel uncomfortable. Indeed, I like to think it gives people permission to be honest about how their own losses have affected them.

When my mom died, a friend who had also lost her mother a year or so before sent me a grief book. It said, in part, that most people tolerate another's grief for about a month (at most). A month seems stingy to me. At one month, I was still barely upright and functioning.

Modern culture is big, big, big on beginnings and small, small, small on endings. People often tilt their questions accordingly. People want you to feel better, so rather than ask, "How are you doing?" it comes out instead, "You doing OK?" because they very much want you to be better. It comes, in part, I think, because people fear what might happen if you are not recovering, and they fear they also might not be OK in a similar situation. Sometimes, I'll say, "The grief remains epic, but I'm still mostly upright."

A couple of weeks after my Heart Dog died, I enjoyed a girl's day out with a childhood friend. We ran into another of my friends at a bookstore and chatted a bit. Later in the day, that friend sent me a text message explaining she hadn't hugged me for fear of triggering a crying jag. To address that worry, I posted a note on social media assuring others that it was safe to hug me. I promised not to fall apart. For the most part, I've been able to keep that promise — even when one of our veterinarians hugged me during a visit to the animal hospital where Lilly died. Oh, I got misty-eyed, but I didn't wail in public or fall to the floor in a heap of grieving goo.

The Tears Will Fall

One of the big misconceptions about the stages of grief is that at some point the crying will stop. Sure, it slows down. You'll probably experience less full-on sobbing or wailing over time, but for me, the crying hasn't yet stopped.

I cried from shock. I cried from regret. I cried from anger. I cried in desperation. I cry now, even as I remember happy times.

Regaining Your Footing

Losing your Heart Dog knocks you off the rails. You feel unmoored, like a ship that has lost its anchor. You'll feel like you're walking on ice or in quicksand.

It takes a while to regain your footing. For some, familiar routines help. For others, it requires major changes in daily life to avoid painful reminders or to create a completely new life worthy of the loss.

In the remaining chapters, I hope you find

realistic and practical strategies for moving forward
— not without grief, but in spite of it.

3
THE EARLY DAYS OF GRIEF

Grief is patient, with a long half-life. If you do not handle each day's allotment of grief, it lies in wait — hitting hard later.

While you might wish for a fast-forward button in life so that you could speed through the most painful parts of grief, the only way forward is through — through the heartache, through the tough times — rather than avoiding them or distracting yourself.

It isn't a new idea. The first mention I could find about getting through life's pain by moving through it comes from a 1914 Robert Frost poem called "A Servant to Servants."

Daily Dose of Grief

I believe each day after the loss of your Heart Dog comes with its own individual dose of grief. Some days the grief falls heavy. Some days it feels a bit lighter, at least for a few moments. I even experience days where I'm crying again mere minutes after thinking to myself that I feel better — if not happy, then at least not desperate.

Grief is patient, with a long half-life. If you do not handle each day's allotment of grief, it lies in wait — hitting hard later. That's why you hear of people falling apart out of the blue, long after the acute grief period. I'm not saying you won't feel ambushed by the grief now and then, no matter what you do, but I believe giving grief the time and attention it requires is necessary for true healing.

That's why it makes me bristle when people recommend distracting yourself from the grief, like keeping busy fixes everything. Many believe that grief becomes seductive, like a sea siren calling you to your doom. They may not say so aloud, but some find grief a form of extreme self-pity, even masochistic or narcissistic. I disagree.

Let me be clear. Grief is not selfish. A naturally occurring phenomenon, grief takes hold in so many ways that simply ignoring it will get you nowhere.

I'm not recommending that you wallow endlessly in your grief. Instead, I simply mean to acknowledge that working through grief requires handling your daily dose of grief one way or another. Today you might cry a lot. Tomorrow you might binge-clean all your closets. Some days you may be desperate to get out of the house. Other days you may loathe the idea of being around people.

Early on, grief work can feel like an all-day thing, but eventually, you'll be able either to set aside time to process your grief or to handle it each time it bubbles up in the moment. Personally, I do a little bit of both. Don't worry if it takes a while to figure out what works best for you.

Below you'll find some insights and advice for the early days of your grief, including four items you need right away.

Grief Day One

If possible, do not work on the day your Heart Dog dies — and the day after, if you can use a sick day or a vacation day. Such a tremendous loss deserves time and space. No one should require you to do anything but survive those first couple of days. Make eating, sleeping, and breathing your goal. That's it. It's fine to retreat into survival mode.

Take more time off, if you can. When my mom died in June 2013, I took three weeks off — her final week in hospice, the week of the funeral, and a week beyond that. Granted, I'm self-employed and have flexibility for such a lengthy leave. I managed it by putting off certain deadlines, asking other writers to fill the gap, and completely canceling some assignments. Maybe you have some sick time or comp time saved up?

Because my Heart Dog, Lilly, died right before Christmas, I found ways to wrap up my final deadlines for the year or to put things off until after the holidays. Essentially, I did not work from December 17, the day Lilly died, through January 5. Many of my clients shut down the week between Christmas and the New Year, so it wasn't a strain for me to be unavailable as well.

I also canceled all holiday plans and stayed home. No shopping. No gifts. No family dinners. No parties. I found it simply too hard to be out in public and to appear normal. I know people who've gone ahead with various kinds of gatherings, only to experience an outburst that made things awkward and potentially damaged relationships.

You'll need to decide what's best for you, but I recommend some quiet time in the early days of your loss.

Grief Week One

Time truly does take on a gelatinous quality when you grieve. Early on, you may find it hard not to mark the passage of time: Less than a day ago, she was sleeping at my feet. Just last week, she was running in the yard. It's Tuesday again. That means she has been gone another week.

Even now, as I'm further from that terrible day than you may be, it feels like just yesterday and forever ago at the same time. Who knows? Maybe grief has a time-travel effect on our hearts, jumping from past to present through the pain.

Grief also feels heavy, as if your body is concrete. Especially early on, you may feel like you're dragging yourself from day to day. Getting a little bit of exercise, even if you don't feel up to a full workout (whatever that is for you), can help. I walk, for example, and it amuses me that no matter how fast or slow my pace seems, my routine walk up the mountain takes pretty much the same amount of time. I always feel better afterward, even if I sobbed the entire time, which I often still do.

Grief alters your perceptions of just about everything — time, things people say, the importance (or lack thereof) of things that once mattered to you. Part of this change stems from a loss of your routine with your Heart Dog. From feedings and possibly giving meds, if your dog was sick for a while, taking care of your Heart Dog provided a rhythm and even a purpose to your days. Without that structure, you may feel lost.

And that's fine. Just keep slogging your way through your feelings and any other demands on your time and energy that first week. Don't expect to be fully functional, but do try to function a little.

Grief Month One

Around the one-month mark, other people will assume you're back to normal. That's about how long modern society tolerates grief in any public way. While the idea that a month is even close to enough time to process the loss of a Heart Dog makes me wildly cranky, I share this threshold so that you won't be surprised when friends and family check out of the situation. You may feel abandoned.

It can be a weird, lonely time because you're still trying to figure out how to go on with your life and perhaps merely staggering through each day like a Grief Zombie. As you get past those first weeks, try to rebuild or recreate some structure to your days so that you can fake it when required, like at work.

Yes, you have to get out of bed most days. If you need a day here and there to wallow, take it, but I encourage you to get out of bed and into the shower. There may be days when you'd rather stay in the shower forever. I do a lot of crying in the shower, and sometimes it helps to be warm in a small space.

You may experience the constant need to sleep or the total opposite with insomnia. It's aggravating, but do your best to honor your body's requirements.

Four Things You'll Need

People say that grief improves over time. In my

experience with other losses of both human and canine friends, that seems to be true. Because I had so much loss in my life for five solid years and because the loss of my Heart Dog eclipses and compounds the others in so many ways, I fear I might never fully recover. I won't, however, give up trying to heal my broken heart.

The rest of the book offers real-world ideas for processing your grief, but I wanted to start with four things you'll need right away.

(1) Grief candle.

If you cannot take much time off or you think it would be better to continue working and meeting other obligations, then I suggest setting aside at least an hour each day to grieve. I mean full-on wailing grief, if you're so inclined.

Get yourself a good, safe candle (like one in a jar). Light it an hour a day while you process your feelings. (Candles remain a leading cause of house fires, so be really careful. Grief also makes us forgetful, and you don't want to forget to blow out your candle.)

My theory is that if you burn this candle daily and give your grief a home, then it's less likely to spill over into your daily life. I cannot promise you won't break down in the grocery store line or other inopportune spot, but knowing that you have set aside time to grieve does help.

Battery-powered LED candles work great for other stages of mourning, but I prefer the ritual of lighting a real candle in the beginning. I also think the symbolism of the candle burning down over time serves as an important measure of your progress toward healing.

(2) Your favorite photo.

With so many digital photos but so few photo prints, you may need to make a special trip to get your favorite photo of your Heart Dog printed. Keeping digital photos on your computer, tablet, phone, or other mobile device is good too, but I recommend having a photo print you can carry around or place in a nice frame at home.

(3) A memento from your Heart Dog.

Choose something that's meaningful to you. Maybe it's your dog's collar or favorite toy. You can either place the item somewhere prominent in your home, like a mantel or shelf, or carry the item with you, if that helps.

For several nights after Lilly died, I slept with her collar or a sweater I knitted for her. I've also strapped her favorite toy (a stuffed monkey) into the passenger seat of my car. It may seem silly, but it gave me comfort in those early days.

(4) A cold, wet washcloth.

Yes, I know it sounds like something you'd do if you were a damsel who got the vapors and needed to lie down on the fainting couch, but it's surprising how much a cold, wet washcloth helps. It gives you a chance to feel more self-contained and calm when your grieving heart is in an uproar. Even if you only lie down for 10 or 15 minutes at a time, with your sore eyes covered, I think you'll find that it helps, especially in the early days.

Grief and Personal Safety

Because grief causes emotional and even physical distractions, be careful in your daily life to protect your personal safety. Amid the upset, it's all too easy to let your guard down and put yourself at risk.

Here's why I worry about the blur of living in a grief-stricken state. A man from New York told his family he was going out to bury his dog and then vanished. Truly. Never seen again. A teenaged girl from Illinois crashed her car and died while fleeing with her dog, who had been diagnosed with cancer. The dog also died in the wreckage. I know a family who experienced a house fire, right after a death in the home, when someone placed oxygen hoses in the laundry room. They forgot to turn off the oxygen tanks, and the heat from the clothes dryer sparked the fire.

Distracted by grief, anyone can make dangerous or fatal mistakes, including becoming a victim of a crime through lack of awareness — out in public, forgetting to lock doors, and such. Please be careful.

Whatever Works for You

Grief is a universal experience. I cannot imagine many people get through life without suffering through — and recovering from — the death of a loved one. While there are some common elements and experiences of grief, you'll need to figure out how to cope with the loss in ways that make sense to you.

I sincerely hope that you find greater comfort and less desperation over time. However, you'll likely experience days three months, six months, or even a year later that feel as hard as or harder than the day your Heart Dog died.

I asked via the grief survey on my *Champion of My Heart* dog blog how long it took to feel "normal" again. Keep in mind people voluntarily took the poll, with the premise that they had indeed suffered the death of a Heart Dog.

The responses give us insights because more than half of the respondents felt better at some point in the first year after losing their Heart Dogs. The takeaway is to hang in there, even in the tough early days. It does get better. It will get better.

How long was it before the acute grief improved and you felt somewhat "normal" again?

- 14% said three months.
- 21% said six months.
- 20% said one year.
- 7% said two years.
- 1% said three years.
- 3% said more than three years.
- 34% said "I still don't feel 'normal.'"

4
SMALL STEPS FORWARD

Do what you can to honor your dog's memory while not erasing all traces from your home.

Try not to panic about reminders of your Heart Dog in your home. You may feel the urge to donate or dispatch your dog's belongings to storage right away. Stay with me here because I'm going to recommend a slower, more methodical strategy for balancing the archiving of your Heart Dog's life with other memorial activities.

It's easier to decide when and how to clean up or put away your Heart Dog's things if you live alone because you can do what feels right to you, and only you. If other family members are involved, however, proceed carefully, and try to respect their feelings. Even the smallest change in the house may feel too big to others who loved her as well.

Figure out what absolutely needs to be done soon for your comfort, but then put off the rest — doing just a little bit at a time over many days, weeks, or months.

For example, my Heart Dog, Lilly, suffered terrible nosebleeds, especially in her final days. She also experienced total incontinence the last 18 months of her life, so I had been doing a lot of laundry, every day, for a long time. When we got home from the hospital after her euthanasia, I washed most of the blankets and bedding. I also soaked and washed my jeans, which were covered in her blood.

I chose, however, not to clean up all of the drops of blood on our tile floors. Lilly and I spent a lot of time sitting in the sun inside the sliding glass doors, including during her final hours. I couldn't bring myself to mop those spots. Instead, I let the drops of blood wear away over time on their own. I did the same with a few tiny blood spots that Lilly sneezed onto my Kindle. To clean them felt like a betrayal.

A few bloody items remain in the house. So far, I have not thrown them away or tried to clean them. The best I can do with some heavy bedding that requires major soaking and a trip to the car wash is to wait until I think I can clean off the blood without it being traumatic. Honestly, I may have missed the window where I could accomplish this task without too much stress. I probably should have done it sooner, but it requires leaving the house, and I had a really hard time being in public in the early days. So, I will advise that you wait — but not too long — to take care of certain things.

Try to find a balance between cleaning up or putting away things that make you sad or that bring up bad memories and the emptiness of not having your Heart Dog's things around the house. Before you move or store items, confer with others in your home. Each time I felt ready to take another step, I checked with my husband first to be sure it wouldn't be too upsetting for him. Lilly was his Heart Dog as well.

A one-to-one ratio worked well for us — especially in the early days and weeks. For every one thing I cleaned up or put away, I spent time working on a memorial project of one sort or another. (See Chapter 5 for ideas on those projects and activities.)

For example, I didn't move any dog beds from our living room until I had a memorial tableau arranged on the fireplace mantel. It features some of our favorite photos, Lilly's favorite ball, her sweater, and a battery-powered LED candle.

It took me months to tidy up Lilly's bedroom. In fact, when my husband asked if he could use that space to store some boxes from his childhood home,

I completely fell apart sobbing. It was really more the shock of the request. By the next morning, when I told him it was OK, he had decided that it was indeed too sad to use the space in that way. Not long after, I spent a solid day organizing our house so that he had a better spot to store his things.

I cannot promise the process will be easy. It won't, but do what you can to honor your dog's memory while not erasing all traces from your home.

Here are a few other trades or compromises you might make:

- Putting away your Heart Dog's bowls only after you've placed memorial flowers in the kitchen
- Carrying your dog's collar with you until you receive ashes back
- Keeping your dog's toys visible when you put away beds (or vice versa)
- Hanging a large photo or painting of your dog in a prominent spot in your home when you've nearly completed your cleaning-up process

It's normal and fine to keep some of your Heart Dog's things out in the open as you do the hard work of processing your grief. Even if your instinct is to put everything away — right away — I encourage you to allow one reminder to remain.

Finding Ways to Feel Better

The grief survey asked people to write about things that made their grief better or worse. In some cases, the answers about feeling better focused on "positive thinking," for lack of a better term. Perhaps repeating these phrases will help, if they apply to your situation:

- My dog is at peace and no longer suffering.
- I did the best that I could for my dog. Nothing more could be done.
- I said goodbye 1,000 times. Nothing was left unsaid.
- My dog died at home, surrounded by her favorite things and favorite people.
- My dog knew I was with her when she died.
- My dog was loved and had a good and happy life.
- My friends understand my loss. I can reach out to them anytime.
- It is normal to grieve this loss.
- Through these personal rituals and remembrances, I honor my dog and our special bond.
- I will remember the happy times and not fixate on the sad ones.

Blog readers who've lost their Heart Dogs also reported finding comfort in these actions or ideas:

- Blasting loud music.
- Coming up with funny statements, like Katy Scofield, who started telling people, "Ben and I were of the same heart and the same brain, so now I'm a broken-hearted half-wit."
- Sending out obituary postcards to family and friends.
- Working with an animal communicator/pet psychic to send or receive messages.
- Spending time with your other dogs or friends' dogs.

Build Your Own Support Structure

Working through your grief may require a whole host of strategies — combined or staged on a certain timeline. Consider ways that you can build a support structure that makes sense for your personality and needs. For some, that may include making a to-do list and checking off your progress. For others, it might work better to write a variety of strategies, tasks, or mantras onto slips of paper. Each time you feel a bubble of grief rising, reach into a big bowl of those ideas and pull one out.

Grief can make you feel like you are lost at sea. Figure out what gives you a point of reference as you sail forward into life without your Heart Dog.

5
MOURNING AND MEMORIALIZING YOUR HEART DOG

Take on memorial projects to focus your grief in productive ways. It's better to embrace your grief through action, rather than ignore it.

There is so much more to mourning and memorializing your Heart Dog than putting together a photo album or scrapbook. That's not to knock that old standby advice, especially if you're a great photographer or avid scrapbooker. I'm just saying to make the most of everything now available to you.

I recommend using these strategies to help lessen the blow of archiving tasks covered in Chapter 4.

Grief Candle

I mentioned a grief candle in Chapter 3, but I want to reiterate the power of this tool. Whenever something bad happens or someone needs love and support, my first instinct is to light a candle.

For me, I suppose, it's an act of intention or mindfulness. When you light the candle or as it burns, you remain rooted in the moment with your focus on your grieving heart or the hearts of others in need. I like the ritual of it.

Grief makes you forgetful and distracted, so please be careful when you have regular candles lit in your house. I come from a family with many firefighters, so I'm cautious — bordering on paranoid — about flames.

The grief candle is essentially a large candle in a safe container that you burn just a little bit of every day. Use it to mark the beginning and end of the time you set aside to grieve.

You may simply sit and cry in the early days. As the months go on, light the candle while you wash and store your dog's toys or when you listen to music that reminds you of your Heart Dog. (See Remembrance Music later in this chapter.)

My theory is that by the time you've used up the candle (remember to get a big one), you'll be feeling at least a little better, a little less desperate.

Eternal Light

If you prefer to have something lit round the clock, buy one of the battery-powered LED imitation candles. Get some rechargeable batteries too because you will go through a lot of them.

The really nice, larger LED candles can cost as much as $50 to $60 each. Since May 2012 when we lost my mother-in-law, we've had one of those lit next to a photo of her and my husband.

After my Heart Dog died, I found an LED candle on clearance for about $6. We keep that one on the fireplace mantel next to some photos and some of Lilly's favorite items. When the rest of the house is dark at night, I like seeing the glow in the living room. I suppose I pretend a flicker of her spirit remains here.

Tribute Video

Today's tribute videos — featuring favorite photos, video clips, and your Heart Dog's theme song, if you have one — eclipse the scrapbooks of old.

It takes quite a bit of time but just a little tech savvy to make a video. If your computer didn't come bundled with video editing software, look online for ways to download something you can use. If your Heart Dog came into your life before digital cameras, you'll also need to get any old photos scanned so that you can import them for your video.

Now, when I say video, it's really more of a slideshow. If you have video clips, great. If not, don't worry. You can use special effects like panning or zooming in or out on photos to make the tribute slideshow a little more dynamic.

Step 1: Gather all the photos and video clips of your Heart Dog.

This can take some time if you've archived photos somewhere other than your current computer hard drive. This process of gathering photos requires you to remember good times, including some you've probably forgotten. It's especially important if your Heart Dog had been sick for a long time. It's good to see visual proof of your amazing canine companion in the prime of life — strong, healthy, happy.

Step 2: Choose your tribute music.

Maybe you have a favorite song. Maybe it's a song that reminds you of your Heart Dog. Maybe it's a song that was popular when your dog was sick or right around the time you lost her. Or, maybe you'll need to look around for a song that aptly conveys her spirit or how you feel.

Consider choosing a couple of songs. One upbeat. One more reflective. You'd be surprised how much music affects the tenor of your tribute video. I tried both Beethoven's "Moonlight Sonata" and Andrew Gold's "Thank You for Being a Friend" for the tribute video I made when my mom died. Let's just say that I was sobbing after the first few notes of the sonata.

It really depends on your intent. If you want something that triggers a good cry, go for it. If you want something happier, then do that. In fact, you may want to create more than one video tribute so that you always have something to watch based on your mood.

During my Heart Dog's long illness, I spent a lot of time in the car with her, driving back and forth to veterinary appointments — sometimes as many as six or seven appointments in five days. I found myself a little obsessed with Mumford & Sons' *Babel,* which won the 2013 Grammy for Album of the Year. I listened to it nonstop in the car for many months. The song "I Will Wait" became sort of an anthem for my life with (and later without) Lilly. I knew I would use that song in her tribute video, long before she died. You can watch the video in the *Rest in Peace* section of ChampionofMyHeart.com or via our *Champion of My Heart* YouTube channel.

Step 3: Match photos to the music.
You'll need to decide if you'll show the photos

chronologically or in some other narrative order. Also, find ways to match certain phrases or changes in the song to your photos.

For example, when Lilly's song says "bow my head," I used a photo where it looks like she is praying over a favorite toy. When the song says, "turn my spirit gold," I used a photo of Lilly smiling next to some golden wildflowers. I also managed, in a couple of spots, to include funny photos of Lilly — biting down on a stick with her eyes squinting and sitting in her kissing booth — right on the beat of the music for emphasis.

Step 4: Decide how to end.

Remember, you're telling a story with your tribute video. It's a story of your dog's life. It's a story of your unique love. Figure out what sort of ending you want in your video. Ideas include:

- Your favorite photo of just your dog
- Your favorite photo of you and your dog together
- A photo of a rainbow
- A photo of a sunset or sunrise

Lilly's tribute video ends with a video clip of her running toward the camera, across a green pasture. She is smiling and has a small stick she had just fetched in her mouth. Even before Lilly got sick, I always knew I would use this clip in this way. To add drama, I added a slow-motion effect. Just as she reaches the camera, the video fades to a rainbow photo that I borrowed from a friend. That becomes a rest in peace message with the dates of her birth and death. Then comes a photo of the clay paw print our veterinary team made for us the day Lilly died.

I still debate showing that paw print and even the rainbow at the end of Lilly's video. I know a lot of people love the Rainbow Bridge pet loss poem. I know some people who hate that analogy. I'm not a huge fan, but I do like that other dog lovers recognize the rainbow reference, so I went with it.

Remembrance Music

Consider putting together playlists of music that help you recall happy times and music that brings emotion to the surface to help your body purge the grief. There is nothing wrong with dancing around your house, remembering joyful times. There is nothing wrong about inducing a wailing cry. Particularly if you made the decision to have your Heart Dog euthanized, Bob Dylan's song "When the Deal Goes Down" from his *Modern Times* album is a proven trigger for sobbing.

I wore headphones a lot in the early days, both at home and in public. I find it helps create a protective bubble. Particularly in the acute or angry stages of grief, other people will bug you.

Everything they do and say may make you cranky. Closing out the world with music can protect you from such intrusions and prevent outbursts.

Photos or Artwork

In Chapter 4, I gave ideas for archiving your Heart Dog's life and items (beds, toys, and such). Once complete, that process creates a renewed absence in your home. That's why I recommend getting your favorite photo or photos enlarged and framed for prominent and permanent display. Original paintings are also a terrific option, if you can afford to have one done by an artist.

My original plan to hang three 8x10 photos in a single frame fell apart when we couldn't find a frame that worked. After such daunting veterinary bills, I also didn't really have the money for custom framing.

Luckily, my husband found a collage-style frame with six photo spots instead of three. We placed our three favorite photos of just Lilly, along with a photo of me and Lilly, a photo of my husband and Lilly, and a photo of Lilly and our elderly dog, Ginko, in the frame. It makes a nice recap of her life. Some of the photos come from before she was sick. Others were taken during her illness.

The frame we chose sits on the fireplace mantel with our memorial candle and a few other items, as

I mentioned earlier. The original plan was to keep it there for a year, then hang it in my home office, but I suspect that it'll stay on the mantle forever.

Graves, Ashes, Urns

Local ordinances often dictate whether or not you can bury pets in your yard. That's one reason some people buy a plot at a pet cemetery. Either way, you can place headstones or other memorial stones in your yard if you'd like.

If you chose to have your Heart Dog cremated, you also have options for how to store the ashes once you get them back. I've chosen to keep all of our dogs' ashes in the house. I created a memorial shelf in my office with each dog's ashes arranged in their boxes, along with my favorite photo of each dog and their collars.

Some veterinary hospitals let you choose from a selection of containers for your dog's ashes. Others opt for a simple one for all dogs. I don't love the treasure chest box that came back with Lilly's ashes, but until I can find something I do love, it works fine. Maybe it will grow on me.

Check out flea markets and antique stores for possible urns or other types of unique containers for your Heart Dog's ashes. I'm sure you could find beautiful art glass containers or distinctive wood or metal boxes that would work well.

Other options include containers for ashes that

look like rocks so that you can place them in your yard or memorial garden, if you have one. Some companies create decorative items that incorporate ashes, like pretty paperweights and such, if you'd rather have something more understated.

Some people choose instead to spread the ashes in a favorite spot. If that's your plan, then it may not matter what kind of container you receive.

Memorial Jewelry

On the advice of one of our emergency/critical care veterinarians, I went on a hunt for memorial jewelry that I could wear daily to keep Lilly close to my heart — especially when I had to be out in public in my grief-stricken state. Even if no one can see it under my clothes, I know it's there, and it brings me comfort.

I didn't realize when Lilly died that some jewelers specialize in memorial jewelry that features etched photos or holds ashes. If you look online, maybe you'll find something you like.

To be honest, I felt rather anxious — almost panicked — about finding the perfect necklace right away. I felt awful the entire time between Lilly's death and the day we picked up her ashes. The fresh loss, the raw emotion, and the endless stretch of time ahead of me without her tore at me horror-movie style. I probably rushed this part of the process.

I'm not sure I've found quite the right piece of memorial jewelry yet, but I have several necklaces from which to choose each day, based on my mood:

- A tiny antique perfume bottle (with some of her ashes inside) that we turned into a pendant
- A tiny antique photo frame (with several photo options) that we also converted from a brooch into a pendant
- A pewter heart-shaped bead that's laced up (like sewing a broken heart back together)
- A silver necklace our dog trainer gave me that says, "Lilly … forever in my heart"
- An industrial-style necklace with metal beads and charms, including a copper heart

One of my *Champion of My Heart* dog blog fans also sent me a memorial bracelet.

You may decide on a keychain or some kind of trinket that you can carry in your pocket. No matter what you choose to wear or carry, it helps to have a memorial talisman or good luck charm, of sorts, to keep with you.

About seven months after Lilly died, I stumbled across a customized jewelry company that sells see-through lockets and little charms to go inside. I really liked them. The same company also sells military dog-tag-like items with inspirational words on them that might appeal to you more.

Our ER veterinarian recommends custom paw-print pendants made from your dog's actual paw print — taken in clay at the time of her passing, a scan of an ink print of the paw, or even a photo of a paw. Companies, then, shrink the print down to jewelry size. The pendant our veterinarian had made when her Heart Dog died is about the size of a nickel. She wears it on a chain around her neck.

Memorial Trees

When we lost our Lab, Cody, to cancer in 1999, we planted a flowering locust tree in his honor. It makes me a little sad that his tree remains at our first house, but whenever I see those trees other places, I think of Cody. We tried planting another locust tree at our current house, but it didn't survive at the higher altitude.

Planting a living thing is a healing gesture in your time of grief. Think about how you'll feel if you move or if something happens to the tree, though.

There are memorial tree programs, where trees get planted as part of reforesting or community planting efforts. Maybe you don't need to see the tree daily. Maybe you simply like knowing that a tree is out there. If so, that could be a good option for you.

Memorial Fundraising

Several of my friends in the dog blogging world have hosted memorial fundraisers for their favorite dog charity. Essentially, you ask others to donate money in honor of your Heart Dog.

The process can be fairly straightforward, if you simply have friends send money to the charity. It's best to alert the charity in advance. You can ask them to let you know how much is raised in your dog's honor and who donated so that you can send thank-you notes yourself. Sometimes tracking the details can be cumbersome, so be prepared for that.

If you want to do something special or specific, like I did, then your memorial fundraiser might get a lot more complicated. I learned many surprising and frustrating lessons in the process of setting up a one-time Lilly's Fund campaign. Several dog charities and community foundations turned me down. Everyone wanted the money. No one could do with the money what I wanted to do in Lilly's memory. It's a long story. I could probably write another book on just that process.

After much research and crying, I ended up creating a crowdfunding project and giving the grants on my own. It wasn't ideal because the money people gave wasn't tax deductible, but it was the only way I could do what I wanted to do. I had specific goals for the fundraiser. I simply couldn't settle for less.

Lilly's Fund Recap

We wanted to raise $3,343, which is the number of days Lilly was in our lives. My husband and I gave $693 ourselves — matching the number of days Lilly survived her illness. That left $2,650 for our family, friends, and *Champion of My Heart* fans to raise.

We reached this goal in just 17 days. I let the campaign linger for many weeks, not quite sure what to do. On a whim, I decided to see if our fans would help raise another $500 in the final five days of the campaign, which ended on what would have been Lilly's 10th birthday.

Once we reached our goals, I alerted the veterinary hospital where Lilly received neurology, internal medicine, and emergency/critical care help. I merely asked our team of veterinary neurologists and veterinary technicians who knew and cared for Lilly to choose canine neurology cases as the recipients of Lilly's Fund grants. I set no criteria, and I am not involved in selecting grant recipients. I trust the hospital to find worthy cases.

Essentially, I use the money to pay someone else's veterinary bill. It's a surprise to the families who benefit — like a random act of kindness. So far, Lilly's Fund has made one grant to a dog with a case similar to Lilly's. More money remains to make additional grants.

I also contacted our main veterinary hospital

and added the extra $500 raised into their "Chip Fund," created in honor of a dog named Chip. They use the money to help people pay large, unexpected veterinary costs. Again, I set no criteria. I simply asked that they give the money to a family with a dog in need.

Do Something

I encourage you to do *something* — actively choose memorial activities meaningful to you. Consider these additional options:

- Raise money to help build a hiking trail (even better if you can petition to get the trail named after your dog).
- Donate a memorial bench or get a bench dedicated in your favorite park.
- Host a food and toy drive for dogs up for adoption in your community.
- Encourage people to help fund veterinary research into your dog's illness.
- Walk, run, or bike in local charity events.
- Plant a memorial garden.
- Sponsor one adoptable dog a month at your local shelter.
- Add a provision to your will to establish some kind of scholarship in your dog's memory.

Unlike when people suggest doing things to distract yourself from the grief, taking on memorial projects focuses your grief in productive ways. It's better to embrace your grief through action, rather than ignore it.

6
COMFORTING THOUGHTS

You will go on in life not without grief
but in spite of it.

It isn't my intent to stir up a theological debate. Instead, I want to offer some ideas that I hope provide new perspectives on grief, no matter your religious background or the status of your personal faith.

Tonglen Meditation

Typical meditation practices tell you to breathe in the good and breathe out the bad. Tonglen meditation, however, suggests doing the opposite. You breathe in the pain of your grief. You feel it in its full, unrelenting glory. Then, you remind yourself that likely millions of other people currently feel the same pain about a loss in their own lives. The universal nature of grief binds you to them. When you breathe out, you release comfort to share with all the others grieving today.

It's a Buddhist idea that all suffering comes from avoiding things we don't want and holding tight to things we do want. The lesson is essentially to accept the good and not-so-good in life with equal measure.

Remember my aversion toward distracting yourself or avoiding grief? Tonglen meditation does the opposite. It instructs you to feel that pain. Really feel it. Then, share comfort with yourself and many others in the same situation.

What I like about tonglen meditation is that it can help you feel less alone. Truly, millions of people grieve today and every day. If you can remember that, I hope you will find both peace and comfort.

Be a Lake, Not a Cup

There is a story that comes out of the Hindu tradition where a teacher explains to a student how best to handle the bitterness in life by comparing it to adding a bunch of salt to a cup of water versus adding a bunch of salt to a large lake. If you drank water from the cup, it would taste terrible because of the concentration of salt in a small amount of water. If you drank water from the lake, however, you wouldn't taste the salt at all. The parable says, "The amount of pain in life remains the same, exactly the same. But the amount of bitterness we taste depends on the container we put the pain in."

You'll need to figure out what being a lake means in your own life. What bigger space, real or imagined, can you use to dilute the pain and avoid bitterness?

For me, this lesson takes the form of long walks or hikes outside. It can be wildly windy where I live. Instead of cursing the gusts that probably make me look like a mime trudging our rural roads, I imagine the wind blowing away my grief. I cry a lot on my walks, but I always feel better when I return home.

I won't kid you. It's difficult for me to walk the same roads and trails where Lilly and I had so many adventures. Even now, various neighbors stop me to ask where Lilly is. We were such fixtures in our community. People wonder.

I walk anyway. I walk not without grief but in spite of it.

For you, being a lake may take a different form, such as running on trails instead of a treadmill or spending more time in your community of faith, taking part in a community theater or community gardening project, or simply spending time with like-minded groups of friends.

The bottom line is that you need to put yourself

in a larger space — mentally, physically, or spiritually. Even if you merely imagine yourself as a lake, that's a start.

Glass Half Full, Glass Half Empty

You know the old joke about optimists saying the glass of water is half full and pessimists saying the glass of water is half empty? Well, it goes a step further. The glass is half full of water and half full of air. It always has been completely full, in that way.

Consider this joke as a representation of our physical and spiritual lives — body and soul, if you will. As the water dwindles, air fills the space, like when the soul leaves the body (if that's what you believe). There is no body now, but everything that once was remains in its entirety, just in another form.

Imagination

Once Lilly became so sick, I tried to memorize her body, her voice, her smells, and everything else about her. I wanted to create visceral memories that I could cling to when she was gone.

I suppose it's a bit like having an imaginary friend as an adult, but I pretend Lilly is snuggling in bed with me when I fall asleep and wake up. I picture her walking at my side on hikes, looking up and smiling. Sometimes, I pretend her spirit has human-like hands and that we're holding hands on my walks. And, yes, I talk to her — all the time. Mostly, I tell her how much I love her. Notice I didn't say *loved* her, in the past tense. I love her. I did then. I do now. I will forever.

It isn't just me. My husband "takes Lilly with him" in the car. He jokes that she is his "lucky Bug" protecting him in bad traffic, turning lights green, and keeping him safe in bad weather. He imagines she is with him so much that I call him a "Bug hog" and give him trouble for making my grief worse by hogging Lilly's spirit. ("The Bug" was one of Lilly's nicknames.)

There is a place for imagination when you are grieving. If it makes you feel better and does not cross over into an obsessive or unhealthy expression (like making *other* people pretend she is there too and getting angry if they won't), then I say pretend all you want.

If you use guided imagery meditations or relaxation methods, there's no reason your Heart Dog cannot join you on beach walks, waterfall swims, or other mind's-eye adventures.

Dreams

Many people believe the loved ones we've lost visit in our dreams. I do enjoy when Lilly makes appearances in my dreams. Sometimes, I have nightmares about her final days, but often it's just an everyday dream, with Lilly doing everyday things. It makes me happy to see her face.

Animal Communicators

I didn't hire an animal communicator after Lilly's death, but I have several friends who have. Some received comforting details and insights for the money spent. Others felt that the results — while nice sounding — were too generic to be true messages from their Heart Dogs. If you choose to hire one, check with people you trust to see which animal communicator comes with a good reputation. I definitely wouldn't want you feeling disappointed or snookered.

Jana Rade, a friend and fellow dog blogger (*Dawg Business*), found that using an animal communicator helped her recover much faster from the passing of her Heart Dog, Jasmine, a Rottweiler. "[The communicator] knew things as if she were with us the whole time, which gave me confidence in what she was saying," Jana says, "assurances that Jasmine was happy and knew how much we loved her and understood why we did what we did, descriptions of how she shed her physical body and was pain free, instances when it was described to me that Jasmine was still with me. She even connected Jasmine and Cookie [a new puppy], and I'm quite sure those two hang out together."

What details from the animal communicator

helped Jana the most? Jasmine knew how loved she was. Her spirit is out there and spending time with Jana.

"She is still around now," Jana says, "And the first thing she did after she shed her physical body was run around in circles. It must have been such a relief not to be bound by the body, and we did get Cookie because Jasmine wanted me to."

Signs

Several people who took the grief survey mentioned that they received a sign from their Heart Dog that everything was OK. At my house, we've come to think of the hummingbirds who frequent our feeders from April to October each year as little angels and signs of comfort from our lost loved ones.

MaryAnn Schiff found her sign while visiting a friend's litter of puppies. MaryAnn did not plan on getting another dog after losing her Heart Dog, Roger, (more than 20 years ago) at a young age to a brain tumor. Just a week after suffering the loss, she and her husband visited this friend. The six puppies thundered around her friend's home — from living room to dining room, down the hall, through the kitchen and back. As MaryAnn sat quietly sobbing, the puppies made another lap through the room. One of them came to a screeching halt, looked at MaryAnn, and came over to put her head in

MaryAnn's lap. While that puppy did go home with the Schiffs and she did help some with the grief, she was not another Heart Dog. But MaryAnn considered the experience to be a sign.

Find Your Glory

I hope these examples help you reframe the hardest parts of your grief experience. If nothing else, use them as the catalyst for finding comfort within your own beliefs and community.

People may tell you not to despair because your Heart Dog will always be with you or will always be part of you or that you'll meet again. I think of it more as your Heart Dog helped make you who you are today, and in that transformation we can find glory, if we look.

7

WHEN GRIEF GETS WORSE,
NOT BETTER

After losing a Heart Dog, 54% of people surveyed
began feeling better in a year or less.

People love to say that only time heals grief. You try to believe it. You wait. You hope. And, yet, tick-tock goes the clock as weeks and months pass with the wall of grief — a chasm, a moat, a crevasse — not shrinking. Three, four, six, 12 months later, it continues to stand between you and feeling anywhere close to normal.

My own impatience with grief typically reaches its peak around the three- to six-month mark. When my mom died in June 2013, after a lengthy illness, I remember complaining in September that my grief only got worse, not better. Friends, years out from their own loss of a parent, advised patience and kindness and gentleness toward the never-ending slog. They promised improvement, just not yet.

The results of the grief survey indicate that a majority of people (54%) began feeling better in a year or less. So, if your loss is more recent, hang in there.

While waiting for grief relief, I realized that the loss of daily routines compounded my loneliness and emptiness.

Veterinary Medicine as a High-Contact Sport

Because my Heart Dog, Lilly, required so much round-the-clock care during her illness — in addition to the three days each week when I visited my mom before she died — most of my friends stopped calling. Invitations of any kind dried up when people realized how hard it was for me to get away for any length of time. Plus, Lilly's veterinary bills remained so extreme that I didn't have much money for fun anyway.

The result? Our veterinarians were practically the only people who called or emailed. Other than the grocery store, the veterinary hospital became my only real destination.

Once Lilly died, all that stopped. The silence staggered me. The truth is that I kind of missed the veterinarians, the technicians, and the client service reps. Other than my husband and cashiers at the grocery story, these veterinary professionals had been my only human contact for so long that it took me a while to recover from the end to that connection as well. This veterinary uncoupling from you and your pet's case can add to your sense of loss.

The End of Caretaking

If your Heart Dog was ill for any length of time, you'll also find a void when the need for constant caretaking ends. The time you gave freely floods back into your schedule and consciousness, and you may find yourself asking, "What do I do now?"

Around here, that meant not doing multiple loads of laundry every day. It meant not running Lilly to the veterinary hospital several times some weeks. It meant not racing home from every single required outing because Lilly needed meds or to be cleaned up or whatever.

While I didn't miss the constant worry, caretaking played a big role in my identity and my life. No longer the dedicated girl taking care of her very sick dog, I had become a person only heavily, heavily grieving her loss. Nothing more. Lilly and I were two peas in a pod, best-best friends, two halves of the same soul. And, without her, I lost sight of myself.

Knocked off my perch, I had to rebuild both

my daily schedule and my outlook on the future. That's a big deal, probably requiring a whole book itself, but here are a few ideas that might help jumpstart your life without your Heart Dog.

Strategies for Getting Through the Road Block

Several times already, I've ranted about how much I dislike the idea of distracting yourself from grief. Instead, please think of these ideas as ways to use reclaimed time and energy to take care of yourself or to do something useful with your grief.

Binge-reading easy books.

Coming from the literature side of academics, I admit to being quite the book snob when I was younger. As grief made reading difficult, if not impossible, I found renewed hope and solitude in books with a much lighter hand and fun narrative. That's not to say true literary fiction doesn't provide an escape. It can. I simply had a better and easier time with books never meant to be more than a good story. This might mean finding a series of books from an author you've never read before, or it could simply be re-reading books you liked in the past. Either way, enjoy.

Binge-watching TV shows or movies online.

I admit this is probably a distraction tactic, but it's also a way to return some enjoyment, if not fun, to your life. Plus, if your Heart Dog was sick for a long time, you probably missed some of your favorite TV shows.

Pick something a little lighthearted if you can. I'm famous for not watching popular shows when they first appear on television — either because I don't have time or don't get the channel. I've learned that if you wait long enough, then you can have many nights, weeks, and months of entertainment without the delay between shows or week-to-week, season-to-season, angst. It's an instant-gratification form of TV because you can just watch and watch and watch.

Getting more exercise.

Trust me. I understand low motivation and feeling like you're made of cement. Try to start or work back into a regular exercise routine, and turn it into a moving meditation on your love for your Heart Dog or how you'll overcome the grief.

Use a mantra or your imagination if it helps. Maybe for you, it's a mantra about strength as you lift heavy weights or one about peace as you hold difficult yoga poses. Maybe you're a runner, and you imagine the sound of your feet on the ground as expressions of love for your Heart Dog.

You might experience fits and starts until working on your health truly becomes part of your routine. That's just fine. Do what you can to maintain or reclaim your time, body, and health.

Eating better.

Stress likely manifests in our relationship with food in one of two ways. Either we eat too much, stuffing our sadness with junk or comfort food, or we feel so awful we cannot stomach anything.

In the short term, neither will cause you too much trouble, but as the grief lingers, I encourage you to find ways to get the right foods into your body most of the time. I'm not saying you cannot sometimes dive into a bowl of ice cream or skip a meal because you just don't feel up to eating, but try to get back into a routine that feeds your body what it needs.

Grieving is physically demanding, and your body needs nourishment to recover from the shock, pain, anger, and desperation.

Reaching out to friends and family.

As I mentioned earlier, I defaulted to "No" during Lilly's illness. Taking care of her took everything I had in me — and many things I didn't. I couldn't be away from the house very long, so invitations dried up.

Grief can make it difficult to be out in public. Partly, it takes energy and motivation to get up and out, then behave as if you are not crushed by grief. Partly, it can be frustrating — even hurtful — to see others happy or doing seemingly frivolous things.

When you are ready, and maybe even before you really want to, work on saying "Yes" when people invite you to do things. I began the deliberate process of getting out more around the five-month mark. You may feel up to it sooner or later than that.

Choose a careful mixture of one-on-one get-togethers, small group activities, and public events to test the waters and see what feels the least awkward. Sometimes that's as good as it gets. Don't set the bar too high for yourself. Try things out, and do what works best for you. Always give yourself an escape plan, in case you begin to feel overwhelmed. Now might not be the time to carpool so that you have sole control of your arrival and departure.

For me, the challenge is equal parts having a hard time being out in public and finding that day's dose of grief waiting for me when I get home. Often, I do fine the day of the outing, but the next few days afterward feel extra difficult. (See Chapter 3 for a discussion of each day's dose of grief.)

Doing Something Useful With Your Grief

If the worse/not better phase of your grief lingers, then I recommend taking on a bigger task to catapult yourself into a future without your Heart Dog.

Charity work (probably not dog related).

I understand the compulsion to channel your grief into charity work in the dog sheltering and dog rescue world. I get it and considered it myself.

If that's truly where your heart lands, then go for it. Maybe fostering dogs, until you're ready for one of your own again, is the right thing. Or, you might find great satisfaction in walking shelter dogs or taking part in the shelter or rescue group's dog training program — since people often consider dogs with good manners more adoptable.

Think about taking a break from your dog-centered life as well. Look at other volunteer options in your community:

- Programs to combat hunger
- Historical sites
- Local museums
- Trail building
- Literacy for adults and kids
- Fitness groups
- Political causes

Big, difficult goal.

A friend who is a veterinary school professor cautioned me against filling the void with more dog-focused activities. In fact, she wasn't keen on me writing this book right away, either.

Her theory is that I needed to take on something that was difficult, took a lot of time and energy, was short-term in nature, and was not related to dogs at all.

The best example is training and running a marathon, if you're a runner. If you're a cyclist, maybe it's riding a century or doing a multiple-day bike tour. If you have always wanted to do a short-course triathlon (or, gasp, an Ironman one), perhaps now is the time to pursue that goal.

It could be something less event focused as well. Is now the time to achieve your fitness goals? Have you always wanted to take a major international trip? Do you have a big unfinished craft or hobby project languishing? Have you always wanted to learn a new hobby or skill? Rock climbing, perhaps?

Honestly, I struggled with this idea because grief and desperation made me not care about anything. I just couldn't come up with any ideas that didn't require more time, energy, and money than I had to give. I hope you'll do better than I did.

The Worst of Times

For some people facing the loss of their Heart Dog, the grief and despair cross over into a dark, dark place. I'd be remiss if I didn't mention it.

Several grief survey respondents noted certain things that made their grief worse:

- Seeing the grief of other pets in the household

- Emotional and physical aftershocks, resulting in the person being hospitalized
- Grief-related sleep problems (Everything seems worse when you're exhausted.)
- Having other people ignore your grief or treat it as abnormal
- Unexpected resentment of family and friends with healthy dogs
- Hearing inconsiderate comments from people, such as "It's only a dog"
- Living alone
- Seeing things in stores that your dog would have loved
- Suffering several deaths in your family or circle of friends before or after your Heart Dog's loss
- Having people ask where your dog is

The darkest times often come if you feel any regret. Several people who took the survey expressed profound regret and guilt. I mentioned earlier that I remain haunted by certain moments from the day my Heart Dog died. I work hard not to fixate on or relive those experiences, but it isn't easy. You may feel stuck in a similar way.

I think the only thing those of us with regrets and guilt can do is believe that we did the best that we could at the time. Things happened. We cannot go back and change them.

When your regrets surface, try reminding yourself of the reasons you made certain decisions — to do or not do certain treatments, diagnostics, or interventions. It's good to engage the logical part of your brain when strong emotions like guilt overtake your mood and thinking.

Those moments changed you, and all you can do now is try to make that a change for the better instead of letting regret destroy you.

Both privately and through the grief survey, people have shared with me their thoughts of suicide in the wake of their Heart Dog's death. It seems those who ponder the idea of their own death fall into one of two camps: Those who believe death will reunite them with their Heart Dogs, and those who simply cannot imagine life without their Heart Dogs. One person, in fact, told me she felt glad that she did not believe in an afterlife and the idea of being reunited with her Heart Dog in death because it likely saved her from suicide.

If you feel suicidal over your Heart Dog's death, now or any time in the future, I beg you to reach out for help. As someone who has weathered the suicide of several friends and seen the aftermath for families, I know for sure that your loss would have an even bigger effect on the people who love you than you're currently feeling over the loss of your Heart Dog.

If you feel really stuck, like you're not making

any progress at all with your grief, or if one or more friends suggest seeking professional help, please find an experienced grief counselor or support group — ideally one that understands pet loss.

8
YOUR NEXT DOG

*There is no set timeline. Only you know the right
time for another dog, if there is such a thing.*

It doesn't take long for the questions about
your next dog to begin after your Heart Dog dies.
Sometimes, people start asking just days after your
loss, or they post links to adoptable dogs for you on
social media.

People don't intend to be pushy or insensitive.
Such inquiries likely come from worry about your
emotional strength and stability. They want you to
feel better fast, and many think a new dog or puppy
is the prescription for what ails you.

Ultimately, the question is twofold: Will you
ever welcome another dog into your life? And how
soon?

Never Again

The first question is huge. Some people indeed find the loss of a Heart Dog so devastating that they swear off dogs forever. I've seen family and friends make this choice, usually in their later years in the midst of suffering many losses. I've also seen friends who didn't grow up with dogs shut down after the loss of their first dog.

Making such a drastic decision is one of many reasons I believe we need to help those grieving the loss of a Heart Dog, or any dog. We need to normalize how people feel and help them find constructive ways of coping with the grief and emptiness in their lives.

Next Dog Timeline

Your answer to the second question likely depends on a number of factors: Do you have other pets currently in your home? If so, what health or temperament issues do they have? Do you live alone? How long will it take you to recover emotionally and, in some cases, financially from your Heart Dog's illness and death? What big life events loom (new job, big vacation, moving, marriage/divorce)?

I know people who made plans for their next dog while their Heart Dog was still alive and others who didn't add a dog to their family for many years. I have friends who adopted a puppy almost right away, and others who've yet to make a move.

A new dog potentially provides both a welcome distraction for many and a boost of much-needed happiness — or a fresh start. Many of my friends also consider loving and caring for another dog a form of tribute to their Heart Dog, including several pals who believe their Heart Dog brought the new dog into their lives.

How soon did you get another dog?

- 14% — less than one month
- 10% — one to three months
- 9% — three to six months
- 11% — six to 12 months
- 10% — one to two years
- 12% — more than two years
- 30% — "I have not yet added another dog to my family."
- 4% — "I do not plan to get another dog."

Notice how, for those who added a dog to the family after the loss of their Heart Dog, the survey responses came out relatively evenly spread. While there is not a major frontrunner, I think the distribution of answers (ranging from less than one month to more than two years) shows how deeply personal the decision is.

I won't recommend a timeline. Only you will know the right time for you, if there is such a thing.

Fear of Not Bonding

No matter how long you wait, I think all of us fear that we either won't be able to or won't allow ourselves to love another dog that much again. Our protective instincts shield our hearts from the chance of experiencing such devastation.

Future Heart Dogs

Yet, most people do welcome additional dogs into their lives. Some respondents to the Heart Dog Grief Survey report having had more than one Heart Dog in their lifetimes.

How many Heart Dogs have you had?
- 37% — one
- 27% — two
- 14% — three
- 22% — more than three

Really, you have two options. Take (or pretend to have) control and make a deliberate plan for when, where, and how you'll add another dog into your life. Or, follow fate's lead and see what happens. People who believe the right dogs find us at the right time take this second option.

9
FOREVER CHANGED

*Faced head on, grief brings depth and
understanding. It transforms us.*

Only those who've loved and lost a Heart Dog
truly understand this unique brand of grief. As your
grief ages, I sincerely hope you settle somewhere
closer to gratitude for the experience of your life
together with your Heart Dog than never-ending
despair.

I chose the word *age* on purpose. I don't
believe grief ever goes away completely. It doesn't
disappear over time. It might feel rounder, less
pointed, but it remains. It ages like wine or cheese
or people. Faced head on, it brings depth and
understanding. The grief transforms us. Just as
living with your canine soul mate likely changed the

course of your life or your development as a better person, the loss brings significant shifts as well.

Remember this reply to questions about how you're coping with the death of your Heart Dog? "I'm forever changed by the loss." I like this statement because it doesn't diminish or belittle the magnitude of the grief. It also gives you ownership of whatever comes from the aftermath of such a loss.

Change isn't necessarily bad. Let's consider some of the possible outcomes from both loving and losing your canine soul mate:

- Greater capacity to love, partner, and bond with others (both people and dogs)
- Good fortune of having this (possibly) once-in-a-lifetime experience with a dog
- Stronger sense of empathy for anyone going through any period of worry, illness, and loss
- Increased knowledge of dog health, behavior, temperament, and other issues
- Better understanding of your own needs when you connect with the dogs, people, and even veterinarians in your life

It's easy to remain mired in the mucky parts of grief. To combat this tendency, make a list of all the ways your Heart Dog made you a better person or the biggest adventures you shared. Refer to it in moments when the grief overwhelms you. Remember those life-changing experiences to balance any lingering regrets.

Well into my Heart Dog's illness, I began putting a penny into a vase every day she survived. I based the idea on a friend's strategy of placing a small stone on a tree stump at the top of a hill every time her ailing dog felt strong enough to walk that far. Because I started the practice late, I went ahead and seeded the vase with enough pennies to represent the days going back to Day 1 of Lilly's illness.

That vase — with 693 pennies inside — remains on the bookshelf in my office. Gratitude pennies, I guess you could call them. I look at them and remember to be thankful for all the extra days we had together. My Heart Dog easily could have died that first day — and on many other days of her illness. Each of those 693 days remains a blessing in my life, along with the total 3,343 days we spent side by side.

Ultimately, the goal is to be all right while accepting that things will never be the same. In handling each day's dose of grief, in finding constructive ways to honor and remember your Heart Dog, in seeking and using comforting thoughts, you can regain your footing and move through the grief — and forward with your life.

I wish you well on your journey.

APPENDICES

Pet Loss Resources

Because phone numbers, web links, and web content can quickly change or become disconnected or out of date, here are some ideas on finding up-to-date pet loss resources any time:

- Ask your primary veterinarian for recommended local pet loss resources.
- Check with the nearest veterinary college. Student volunteers often run free pet loss hotlines.
- Search online for the terms "grief" or "pet loss," along with the name of your nearest city or town.
- Check out the Association for Pet Loss and Bereavement online.
- Search online booksellers for pet loss, sorting by popularity or publication date.

- Contact local grief support groups to see if they offer any that serve those who have lost pets or whether or not people grieving pets are welcome at regular support group meetings.
- Talk to your own physician about your grief, especially if you feel that it's affecting your physical or mental health.

You'll notice, I'm sure, that I've not listed additional pet loss books. Here's why: I didn't want to be influenced by what's already out there, so I didn't read any pet loss books before writing this one. I simply wrote from my heart and from my experiences, with great input from *Champion of My Heart* readers and fans.

Pet Memorial Resources

A poll of *Champion of My Heart* blog fans and readers revealed an aversion to me naming specific pet memorial products and companies in the book — too commercial and icky, people felt. Instead, here are tips on the kinds of items you'll be able to find. If you are keen on using local resources and services, simply add your location (city/town) to your string of online search words:

- Memorial jewelry (mostly necklaces, but also bracelets, beads, and such)
- Lockets (look for the neat, see-through ones that hold charms)
- Custom paw-print jewelry
- Dog-themed urns for ashes
- Artists who specialize in pet portraits
- Pet memorial idea boards on Pinterest
- Dog memorial donations

Champion of My Heart — **Heart Dog Grief Survey Results**

Q1: How many dogs have you lived with in your lifetime?
541 total respondents
>   1 to 3 (16%)
>   3 to 5 (18%)
>   5 to 7 (19%)
>   More than 7 (47%)

Q2: How many Heart Dogs have you had?
519 total respondents
>   1 (37%)
>   2 (27%)
>   3 (14%)
>   More than 3 (22%)

Q3: How recently did you lose your Heart Dog?
488 total respondents
>   Less than 3 months ago (13%)
>   3 to 6 months ago (8%)
>   6 to 12 months ago (10%)
>   1 to 3 years ago (20%)
>   3 years ago (11%)
>   More than 3 years ago (38%)

Q4: Was your loss sudden or after a longer illness?

464 total respondents

    Sudden accident or illness (52%)

    Longer illness (48%)

Q5: How long was it before the acute grief improved and you felt somewhat "normal" again?

474 total respondents

    3 months (14%)

    6 months (21%)

    1 year (20%)

    2 years (7%)

    3 years (1%)

    More than 3 years (3%)

    Still don't feel "normal" (34%)

Q6: How soon did you get another dog?

463 total respondents

    Less than 1 month (14%)

    1 to 3 months (10%)

    3 to 6 months (9%)

    6 to 12 months (11%)

    1 to 2 years (10%)

    More than 2 years (12%)

    Not yet added another dog to my family (30%)

    Do not plan to get another dog (4%)

Q7: How would you describe your grief over losing your Heart Dog compared to other dogs you've lost?
440 total respondents
>This is my first dog loss. (13%)
>2 x more grief (14%)
>10 x more grief (37%)
>100 x more grief (36%)

Q8: Tell us your gender:
473 total respondents
>Female (93%)
>Male (7%)

Q9: Tell us your age:
487 total respondents
>Under 30 (8%)
>30 to 50 (48%)
>Over 50 (44%)

Survey was live on dog blog *Champion of My Heart* from March 25 to April 1, 2014.

ACKNOWLEDGMENTS

I would be a different person if my Heart Dog, Lilly Elizabeth Hawn, hadn't come into my life. You remain my love, my life, my inspiration, puppy-girl. I feel you in my heart, but I miss you every day.

Never-ending thanks to my husband, Tom, and Lilly's canine contemporary, Ginko, for being the Best Boys a girl like me could want. You have been my lifeboat in the rough seas of grief.

Big welcome and thanks to our new Border Collie puppy, Clover Lee Hawn. Loving you has not lessened my grief, but I know for sure I'd be even more desperate without you at my side.

Big shoutout to my sister, Teresa Carlson. Through all the illness and grief on many fronts, I value our love and collaboration as Beacons of Light (and awesomeness).

Thanks to Hilary Lane, who approved our adoption of Lilly from the Humane Society of Boulder Valley. I value your input and wise counsel. Through this book, I hope I can return the favor as you face your own recent losses.

Much gratitude as well to our dog trainer, Gigi Moss, who we love like a sister and who never gave up on me or Lilly.

Big doses of hopping happiness to my agility friends — JoAnn McDermott, Betsy Harrison,

Cathy Lester, Don and Lori Hansen — who've been so kind even though Lilly and I never did compete.

Lilly's life could have ended differently and suddenly if not for the availability and expertise of our entire veterinary teams at Table Mountain Veterinary Clinic, Wheat Ridge Animal Hospital, and Veterinary Referral Center of Colorado.

In particular, I want to recognize the neurology veterinary technicians — Danielle Boisvert, Daryl Makosky, and Angelika Sherman — for their help throughout Lilly's illness and for coming to say goodbye to Lilly on that last day.

I send much appreciation to Lilly's primary veterinarian, Dr. Donna Valori. Thank you for always letting me think out loud and for helping me make the big decisions.

Lilly's final year would have been drastically different without the leadership and epic compassion from our veterinary neurologist, Dr. Rainier Ko. Thank you for making time for me and Lilly, taking my calls, answering my emails, and providing keen input even on your days off. You didn't have to jump into the raging river midstream. I'm thankful that you did. The insights, tools, and options you gave me made the hard road a little easier. By the time we met, we knew Lilly's story wouldn't end well, but we faced it together just the same. Thank you for that and for your ongoing friendship.

I would have been lost without Dr. Stacy Meola, our veterinary emergency/critical care specialist, in Lilly's final weeks and on that last day. Thank you for being there with us and for us in those final moments. I'm sorry that you had to play a role in our Big Sad, but if it had to be anyone, I'm glad it was you.

A writer goes nowhere without readers. Unending thanks to the readers and fans of the blog — *Champion of My Heart*. I am so grateful that you found Lilly's story, my story, of value in your own life. We were just a couple of girls doing the best we could, no matter what came. Your interest and support buoyed me at the darkest times. Your financial help in the early days of Lilly's illness made the difference between impossible and possible. Thank you.

I thank my fellow writers and mentors on all sides and facets of my career. It all begins with Leslie Petrovski and Lisa Metzger, who helped me get my first writing and editing job, right out of college. It continues with Hilda Brucker because it's always good to have a friend you can tell anything. I'm so thankful to have a cadre of funny, smart, creative, and successful writing mentors who give insights in good times and bad. Thank you, Vera Badertsher, Jane Boursaw, Alisa Bowman, Kerri Fivecoat Campbell, Sandy Grabbe, Donna Hull, Claudine Jalajas, Heather Larson, Sheryl Kraft,

Jennifer Margulis, Melanie McMinn, Ruth Pennebaker, Meredith Resnick, Brette Sember, and the one who brought us all together, Stephanie Stiavetti.

Many thanks to my friends and fellow dog bloggers in the tribe for keeping me emotionally afloat in the darkest times: Amy Burkert, Kim Clune, Vicki Cook, Mel Freer, Peggy Frezon, Mary Haight, Edie Jarolim, A. J. Postiglione, Leo Scheltinga, Kim Thomas, Pamela Douglas Webster, and Christie Zizo.

Much appreciation to the book's beta-readers for offering keen insights into the holes and excesses in earlier drafts: Diane Carlson, Sue Chase, Leland Dirks, Tom Hawn, Stacy Meola, Kari Neumeyer, and Shara Rutberg.

ABOUT THE AUTHOR

Lilly and Roxanne, November 2011, about 2 months before Lilly became sick.

Roxanne Hawn began blogging about her Heart Dog/canine soul mate, Lilly, in April 2007. A real-time memoir, the blog — called *Champion of My Heart* — chronicled life with a brilliant, sensitive dog. Then, things became complicated following Lilly's rare adverse rabies vaccine reaction. The fight for Lilly's life lasted 693 days. Lilly died December 17, 2013.

This book stems from that experience. Roxanne's recovery from the profound loss remains ongoing.

A word-girl since childhood, Roxanne has been a writer/editor her entire career. She spent many years writing for newspapers and magazines. Roxanne began writing professionally about pets in 1995, while working for the American Animal

Hospital Association and later for the American Humane Association. During this period, she served on the board of directors for the National Council on Pet Population Study and Policy (a coalition of animal welfare groups that funded studies into the causes and solutions to dogs and cats ending up in animal shelters). Roxanne also volunteered for many years at an animal shelter, where she witnessed firsthand what happens when the human-animal bond breaks or never forms.

Having shared her life with dogs since birth, Roxanne found herself unprepared for the magnitude of grief after Lilly's death. She has loved all the dogs in her life. She loved Lilly more than words can convey. Heart Dogs are different. The loss felt galaxies worse than Roxanne expected, and that's saying something because Roxanne was born with a good imagination.

A journalist, writer, copywriter, and blogger, Roxanne works from the Rocky Mountains of Colorado, USA, where she lives with her human soul mate, Tom; an elderly Lab + Greyhound named Ginko; and a new Border Collie puppy.

About nine months after Lilly's death and the day after she sent a draft of this book off to beta-readers, Roxanne saw a Border Collie puppy online who was up for adoption. Roxanne could not resist. This puppy spoke to her heart. It took 10 days, countless emails and phone calls with the rescue group, a 1,600-mile journey, a whole lot of faith and fate, even more luck, and at times seemingly half the population of the Commonwealth of Virginia … but 15-week-old Clover arrived in Colorado on September 13, 2014, and has taken on the role as the new canine heroine in Roxanne's life.

Even though it takes an absurd amount of time, Roxanne maintains an active online presence. She is pleased to hear from readers and fans in any of these venues.

Blog: **ChampionofMyHeart.com**

Twitter: **@roxannehawn** and **@champofmyheart**

Facebook: **Facebook.com/championofmyheart**

YouTube:
YouTube.com/user/championofmyheart

Pinterest: **Pinterest.com/champofmyheart**

Please subscribe to the blog or follow Roxanne online for news about additional books based on Lilly's life and for updates on new puppy, Clover. Oh, the stories we may tell.

Roxanne and Clover, December 2014

HEART DOG

88680519R00062

Made in the USA
San Bernardino, CA
15 September 2018